TREASURE AT THE
BOTTOM OF
MY GARDEN

GW00492757

JUDY ROBLIN

Matador
9 Priory Business Park,
Wistow Road, Kibworth Beauchamp,
Leicestershire. LE8 0RX
Tel: 0116 279 2299
Email: books@troubador.co.uk
Web: www.troubador.co.uk/matador
Twitter: @matadorbooks

ISBN 978 1789017 953

British Library Cataloguing in Publication Data.
A catalogue record for this book is available from the British Library.

Printed and bound by CPI Group (UK) Ltd, Croydon, CR0 4YY
Typeset in 11pt Times New Roman by Troubador Publishing Ltd, Leicester, UK

Matador is an imprint of Troubador Publishing Ltd

For the Tymawr family
With thanks and love for more
than forty years of belonging.

We are all called into the deep
by God's dream for us

Fr Daniel O'Leary

A bird doesn't sing because it has an answer;
it sings because it has a song.

Maya Angelou

CONTENTS

THANKS:

To my editor, Annabel Robson, who has accompanied the manuscript every step of the way.

To Anna Tynan for the sketches and Paula Tynan for the cover design.

Also to Chris Griffiths for his initial typing of the manuscript and to Margarate Howells for her encouragement to publish.

FOREWORD

This is Judy Roblin's third book. There is a growing assurance about her writing – a kind of confidence, an inner authority which is forged in 'the smithy of the soul'. When it comes to spiritual guidance there is no substitute for pain and prayer. The evidence for this truth flows throughout the book. Every page has an authenticity and a searing honesty inscribed on it. The twelve chapters are all tinged with intense memory, suffering, pathos, profound depth and mystery. All the predominant graces, experiences and qualities of a lived life, of a seeking human being, of a stripped heart are there – the isolation, the despair, the fear, the praying, the listening, the stillness, the healing, the hoping, the dawning, the gratitude. All the signposts and markers along the journey of a maturing soul have been experienced and honoured by the author.

It is honestly, humbly, convincingly written, every conversational word well chosen. The author borrows colourful and poetic expressions from those writers she admires and respects, and weaves a beautifully-patterned tapestry that sheds light on our own hidden fears and dreams, a light that nourishes the seeds of holiness in our souls. That this transformation happens is due, in no small way, to the sincerity and integrity of the writing. She senses beauty everywhere and writes with a palpable joy about it – emerging through the senses, songs, seasons and shadows. Above all, her suggestions and observations are unfailingly deeply coloured by her understanding of the revealed Christian teaching – the closeness between nature and grace, between the visible and the invisible, heaven and earth, between God and God's creation. Judy Roblin has learned the craft of Incarnation.

There is nothing contrived about the content of the book. It is home-spun wisdom by a wife, mother and grandmother honed in a wee shanty at the bottom of her garden. It is full of the author's own words, own poetry, own experiences, own insights and own faith. And there's a striking simplicity to the drawings. That is why the whole creation will give courage and hope to so many people who are trying to recover from any of the many shades of darkness they have endured, who struggle to recover the light they once rejoiced in, who yearn for the promised abundant life. The author's story and her wisdom will provide the reader with the graced strength and the blessed confidence to let go of much, to believe again, to forgive from their heart, to be patient, to accept, to begin their lives anew and to evolve at God's speed and timing.

Judy is a safe guide as we traverse the labyrinths of our hearts. She is safe and sure-footed because she has meditated on her sufferings, contemplated them in the presence of the Holy Spirit, and shaped them, in her beloved *poustinia*, in the light of the wisdom of some of her favourite spiritual authors such as Harry Williams,

John Robinson, Antoine de Saint Exupéry, Gerard Manley Hopkins, Annie Dillard, Cynthia Bourgeault and Richard Rohr. She reaches for the depth in everything, which, of course, is the incarnate home of the divine presence. And she keeps digging, in all seasons, in the soil of her garden for the twelve spiritual treasures she shares with us and with the world in a spirit of great generosity, humility, vulnerability and confidence.

> An empty shell on a deserted beach,
> I wait with the others who wait
> for the sure tide of your love
> which will come
> and sweep us away
> with the wild wonder of your wanting us.

Fr Daniel O'Leary

PREFACE

oustinia (pronounced 'pou' as in 'you') is the Russian word for desert, *Saharskaya Poustinia* meaning 'the Sahara Desert'. Within the tradition of Russian Orthodoxy it came to mean a quiet, lonely place that people might wish to enter to find God, who is within them; a place where the noise of soul and intellect became silenced and a great 'listening' was able to take place. At the beginning of the fourth century this was one of the standard ways, especially in the East, in which Christian contemplation expressed itself and carries connotations of the Desert Fathers and Mothers of that time.

Essentially then a place for silence and listening, a *poustinia* was a small, sparsely furnished cabin away from, or on the edge of, a village. Taking different forms, some were completely away from humanity, embodying complete solitude, while the majority were still considered to be part of the community. The *poustinik* (the one who entered the *poustinia*) was always able to be called upon if needed. For example, if required to help with the harvest, he would drop everything and respond immediately. The villagers were happy to have him living at the edge of their village and accepted him and his life gladly as a normal and natural way of living. He was not in the *poustinia* for himself. His was an offering of self for the benefit of others through a life of prayer and love.

It was in the early 1960s that a Russian woman, Catherine Doherty, was inspired to incarnate the idea of *poustinia* in the United States. A seeker of silence and solitude, she had established a lay apostolic family in Ontario, Canada, which grew into the Community of Madonna House, still active today. Yet constantly she kept thinking of *poustinia* and whether or not this tradition could be applicable to the West. Then one day, walking in the Community grounds, she passed an old deserted farmhouse and was struck by the idea that this could be transformed into the first *poustinia* of Madonna House. Responding to what she recognised as the impetus of the Holy Spirit, this was the beginning of a seed that would grow beyond her imagination.

Catherine was aware from the beginning of the difference between the *poustinia*s of Russia and what was happening at Madonna House. 'Times have changed and the ways of mankind have changed. The world has become urbanised. But all the more then, is the need for solitude, for the silence of God away from the traffic and all the other noises.' She became aware over time of *poustinia* developing to include not only those wishing to make it a full-time vocation, but those called to a mixed kind of solitude. People began to appear at Madonna House wishing to enter the *poustinia* for a week, a month or a year. 'Perhaps that's the way it should be; perhaps that's the way God wants it to be in these different days.' However, she was adamant the *poustinia* must never simply be a place of rest, of sleeping or recreation. Neither should it be a place for dropping in for coffee. It is God's place and should never be used for anything else but consciously being with him. Catherine wrote of the tradition and of her experiences in resurrecting it in the West in her book called simply 'Poustinia', which has become a spiritual classic.

In *The Language of Silence* a book in the series, 'Traditions of Christian Spirituality' (Darton, Longman & Todd) Peter-Damian Belisle, a Camaldolese monk, speaks of great lovers of solitude, including Catherine Doherty. 'Catherine felt as though she were God's bird sent out to tell the good news to the entire universe. Her ministry strove to open up contemplation's door to everyone, suggesting the way of the *poustinia* for all.' Catherine helped to make monastic solitude and silence accessible to everyone and tried to make contemplation part of everyone's vocabulary. He goes on to say that with his mind's eye he can see thousands who, through her *poustinia* book, are drawn to make silence part of their lives. He can look into homes and see *poustinia* rooms set aside for prayer and is amazed at the *poustinia*s people have built on their personal property.

Today 1300 websites deal with *poustinia* and there are several large retreat centres world-wide where *poustinia*s are available. And I – an ordinary wife, mother and grandmother – have one at the bottom of my garden! How and why has this come about? Certainly it has not simply arrived out of the blue, but is the culmination of a life-long journey and feels like giving birth to something carried within for a very long time.

INTRODUCTION

In *The Alchemist*, Paul Coelho tells the story of Santiago, an Andalusian shepherd boy who travels the world in search of the treasure of his heart, only to discover it, in the end, buried in his own back yard.

This is a parable of my own story and that of so many others who are drawn to pursue the Divine light as it propels us onward through the events and experiences of life. Perhaps it is easier to catch sight of this thread following our footsteps as we look back on our life from the perspective of age. Ruth Burrows has said 'One long searching look into my past and I see there, in its depth, the face of Christ gazing back at me'. I can resonate with that, seeing it all beginning at nine years old when I first became conscious of the loving approach of the Divine. A hunger for further relationship with and understanding of this spirit has accompanied and underpinned the rest of my life, a journey taken both within and beneath the surface of everyday living. Each one of us has their own story and we are fortunate if we find another willing to listen to the telling of it, and help us see the significance of what may lie hidden.

Looking back, I recognise that the carriage of life has been drawn by the two horses of marriage and monasticism.

Neither has been exclusive of the other, but together they have brought life, energy and a way of travelling. Both have provided the stability necessary for freedom and growth, and both have love as their raison d'être. From within a loving marriage, it was yet a time of personal breakdown that washed me up at the door of Tymawr, a Community of Anglican sisters, living a life of prayer based on the Rule of St Benedict. Welcomed and received with love, I found here the unconditional acceptance we all seek: falling in love with the place, the people, and the spirit of Christ which was transparently recognisable. It was here, on an early visit, that I first came across Catherine Doherty's book, *Poustinia*, which even then excited and fired my imagination. From this vantage point of age, it is possible to see that once the two shelters of marriage and monasticism were in place, the real wilderness years began. Accompanied by a loving husband, there followed many years of failure, suffering, contradiction and the darkness of deep depression. This was treated very differently almost half a century ago, involving hospitalisation and heavy drug therapy. 'Everything belongs', says Richard Rohr, and I now see those times of living in the same ward as people with severe mental health problems as part of the novitiate for the *poustinia* of today.

Even then, inexplicably, and alongside and beneath the pain, remained a deep awareness and acknowledgment of the Divine presence in everything that was happening. I mention all this because of today's belief that darkness of some kind is a necessity for growth. We plant a seed in the depth of the earth, where it then germinates if other conditions prove right for its growth.

That first visit to Tymawr proved pivotal to the rest of my life. Thrown in at the deep end into an all-embracing pool of silence, there was no opportunity for fear, only experience of 'underneath are the ever-lasting arms'. My relationship with the Community has remained continuous and constant to this present day. A base within which, and from which, to explore the hidden layers of silence – and latterly solitude – in a growing love affair with the Divine. But should I be writing about a love affair? – I ask myself. However, this lover is not only mine but everyone's, the ground of the being of all people. So I am writing not only of myself but what is true for every person. We all need room to breathe and expand.

Poustinia is a way to freedom, where we are not trapped in passing trivia but become free to be the people we really are. If we are to become fully rounded human beings who offer hospitality of heart to others in the market places of today, we need times of silence and solitude. Only when we are connected to our own inner core can we really connect with others – and the easiest route to this is solitude. For most people it may be a question of being open to opportunities as they present themselves, for example a journey to or from work, being stuck in a traffic jam (if we can curb our impatience!), walking the dog, or being alone in the house when the children have gone to school. I am still struggling to articulate solitude. Somehow it is not the same as silence and prayer. Only having journeyed here in recent years, I think I need to live it a lot more before being able to talk much about it. All I am at present aware of is the experience from within, and I can try to share that. I have been asked why the *poustinia* in my garden is different from prayer in the corner of a bedroom, and without discrediting the latter, which I have done for most of my life, time spent in the *poustinia* is more free. There is room for the spirit to dance, to fly, to lose itself in the ocean of love encountered there. It is a place where lovers meet and can relax completely without fear of distraction or interruption, a place where there is freedom to be completely oneself. Somehow this also involves a physical departure and subsequent arrival, hence the path between cottage and *poustinia* is significant.

Ours is the middle one in a crescent of Pembrokeshire cottages, opening at the back to a 200 metre garden with a stream at the bottom. On the other side of the stream is a nature reserve backed by tall trees. It is the perfect place for a *poustinia*. A winding gravel path in light stone, lined with primroses, leads from the cottage, which I follow every morning on rising. The path is important because it unites both ends of itself into one. Love, energy, life and prayer flow up and down, making the cottage and *poustinia* one whole expression of living. The latter is a simple wooden hut, with windows to the floor at the front and sides allowing full view of the stream and woodland beyond. A small window at the back allows the sun to shine through, while inside, following the tradition of simplicity, is a wicker chair and table with pen and notepad. There is a shelf for an icon written for me by a dear friend, with space for an intercession book. The icon is of Mary and tradition says that she continues the praying when I am not there. A small African china cross stands against the window, while a transfer of Caldey's 'tree of life' shines through it. A small hand-held globe helps to keep vision world-wide, and a wooden plaque of Kahil Gibran's words 'Accept the seasons of your heart' often inspires and could have been another title for these thoughts. For winter months there is a small gas heater, and hook to hang a wet coat. Each morning, whatever the weather, I carry my coffee down the path. What happens is difficult to describe, because mostly nothing happens! Yet there is encounter as I make myself available and open to the beating heart of the Divine in nature, our world, and the depth of myself.

It is interesting that the English word 'solitary' means 'to be alone', but in Russian means 'to be with everybody', and it is this thought that strikes me when I first settle down in the *poustinia*. I am immediately aware of belonging to a community of soul friends, friends of the heart, who meet on the prayer-waves in support and love of each other. Sister Rosalind from Tymawr has spoken of a golden thread running between the *poustinia* and the Community which is a very helpful and encouraging image. This leads to further awareness of journeying with people around the world whom I do not know, but who walk the same path; people of the deep, holding the world before God. Out of this rises a gentle sense of belonging not only to these, or even the natural family of husband, children and grandchildren, but to the wonder of Nature laid out before me, and to our world at large. There is awareness of being part of it all, because of being present in this place.

Simultaneously with the beginnings of life in the *poustina*, I have planted a garden. It is part of the life of this place and a wonderful aid in remaining grounded. In her beautiful book, *Spiritual Gardening*, Peg Streep says 'We transform our gardens and yards into sacred space when we understand them as places of growth not only for plants or trees, but for our inner selves'. The garden is planned on old monastic lines, with four large square borders of cottage garden plants, headed by a round bed of herbs and annuals near the cottage. With no plans to over-control the garden, I hope to learn from the plants themselves where they are happiest and what they like to be near to.

The tradition of *poustinia* demands that the user accept the responsibility to communicate something of what is received whilst present within it. So, as I reluctantly accept the challenge of sharing an experience that is essentially beyond words, I invite you to accompany me through the seasons of the year with the notes I have made along the way. In the original book Catherine speaks of her personal visits to the *poustinia* by elaborating on a single word that she receives while there and which colours and defines that time. I have found this to be an authentic approach and I shall try to follow her example. Initially deeply resistant to speaking of personal experience, I find reassurance in the words of Richard Rohr: 'The place in you that seems to be the most intimate is in reality the most universal and global in scope'.

January

LETTING GO

Waiting

One no-sunshine day
when clouds hang heavy
over the cold-clad earth,
I stand with the sycamore
suspended between times
stripped
naked
in this low life-less air
and wait.

Wait
and listen
for life that lies low
hidden
beneath the surface of things,
for sunshine
and the sap that will rise
full-flowing and free again
through the stark silhouette of ourselves.

The world is white with frost as I walk the path to the *poustinia* this morning; the backcloth of skeletal trees more beautiful than ever with frosted branches glistening in the early morning light. The moon is still up and I think of the tides pulled by its force which change the direction of the stream's flow twice daily. So ordered and full of wonder! An air of mystery holds everything in stillness as I light the fire and settle in the *poustinia*.

Windows are frost-fingered but will soon clear as the space warms, so I will be able to look out from within the womb of surrounding nature.

Today, Nature is at peace in her nakedness, having lived through the processes of growth in Spring, the flowering and letting go of beauty in Summer, and the glory of Autumn. If only our human 'letting go' was achieved so naturally! In his beautiful book *Falling Upwards*, Richard Rohr describes this very process and helps us become aware of it in our own lives. He points out that we spend the first half of our life accumulating all manner of things that help or please us. We build a life by following a certain career path, perhaps getting married, owning a house, having children, building a reputation, serving and making a difference. All very necessary at the time of our development as people. Then, at some point, the season turns, and life appears to change. Either through the natural process of ageing, or through life events such as ill health, bereavement or redundancy, a time of letting go arrives which proves to be easier for some than others.

I would suggest we have been schooled in this practice from an early age; as a toddler we first let go of our mother's hand to stand alone, then we start school, then leave home, or start a job, or a family. Examples fall over themselves so much so that it would seem life has been specifically set up for us to experience what feels like loss in letting go, yet which carries within it possibility of future growth. But still we do not like it! Experience teaches we are not in control of the important events of our lives and this is what we struggle with. Such is the spiritual journey taken by most people, even when it is not recognised as such. For it comes to everyone wrapped up in ordinary events personal to ourselves, so that we all have our stories of when circumstances forced us to let go of something or someone dear to us.

Today it is gratitude that rises when I think back on early-life illness and disappointment. What seemed dramatic, tragic even, at twenty is seen through the years as gift and the beginning of learning to let go and allow God to take control. It felt far from this at the time, when transition from university to psychiatric ward was like the end of the world. The deepest pain, I recall, came not from shame or sense of failure (though that too) but in no longer being of any use to God or man. Plans were shattered, as was any vision of the future. Only Milton's 'On his Blindness' helped:

> Thousands at his bidding
> Speed and post o'er land and ocean
> Without rest,
> They also serve
> Who only stand and wait.

And there was a lot of waiting to be done. Subsequent long years of depression were dark, yet proved to be the cauldron in which my relationship with the Divine was forged and defined. Also, alongside letting go of future plans, came an equally painful letting go of importance and learning not to be afraid of not being anybody special. This was hard after being brought up to excel, yet the dramatic suddenness of this part of the journey cut short a process which could have taken a life-time to realise. I understand Jesus' temptation in the wilderness to take on celebrity status. In the past, visiting old friends who live comfortably with achievement, I have sometimes thought 'What if... I might have been... succeeded... achieved more', but today there are no regrets, for what came wrapped up in the pain was the greatest gift of all ... friendship with the Divine.

Possibly one of the reasons this further gift of *poustinia* has materialised in later life is because it takes some of us a life-time to finally accept the woundedness we carry within, before letting go of our brokenness and stepping over it into freedom. At times of personal darkness friends and guides are invaluable and we often need to trust a human face before we can the Divine. I think here of those who have been with me in times of distress, as well as those who nurtured the flickering light within through

6

personal contact and the written word. They have been many. Whenever support was needed it came in the form of a soul-friend to walk alongside me, and I hold them close with gratitude and thanksgiving.

However, I am now experiencing a new form of 'letting go', glimpsed for some time but clearly sensed in the silence of the *poustinia*. That is letting go of any residual dependency on another person. Having received so much from others and only slowly learned to trust my own soul, this feels like letting go of ties and moving out into the deep. Looking to others for guidance is healthy and natural but can become addictive, and this appears to be a significant moment. Lao Tse expresses it beautifully: 'Always we hope someone else has the answer, some other place will be better. Some other time it will turn out. This is it. No one else has the answer. No other place will be better, and it has already turned out.' Here in the *poustinia* there is no human guide and by now I recognise that trusting God involves trust in one's own deepest self. That long time of wonderfully wise teachers can still be appreciated if I am no longer dependent upon them.

'Letting go' so underpins everything in the world of the spirit, yet I know my needs for human support will arise again. However, for the moment I am content to let go of all thoughts and enter the silence of presence that enfolds me here: wanting nothing, everything found in the mystery of this present moment.

February

ACCEPTANCE

Accept the Seasons of Your heart

K. Gibran

The Tree

The most beautiful tree I have ever seen
stands erect against the elements,
stripped naked against a cloudless sky,
at home in her belonging.
Bark bare in beauty
she speaks from the other side of suffering
of life lived sheltering loss,
of holding Winter with Spring in her branches,
and your absence and presence as one.

February, the lowest time of the year for soil and for soul. One low-energy morning, I venture down the path in darkness, through biting wind and torrential rain. Nature is noisy today; even the stream, risen to river level, races darkly past on its way to the ocean. But once inside the *poustinia*, relieved of wellies and wet clothes, and with the fire warming my frozen fingers, I settle into an oasis of calm to watch and wonder.

The little wooden plaque of Kahil Gibran's quotation, 'Accept the seasons of your heart' jumps out at me and I marvel at this intrinsic quality in Nature itself. It is the sycamore outside the window that speaks. Today is wild but beautiful, a natural part of the seasons of the year. It is as if it says, 'This is how it is today and this is how I am, buffeted by the weather, branches flaying, but my core, rooted in the ground beneath me, is secure.' If only this were so for us! If only we could face each season of life, whatever the weather, with such acceptance and empathy with the way of things. Soon it will be Spring and will begin again the cycle of transformation. Is it too much to believe the same is so for us? In *The Silent Land* Martin Laird uses the analogy of mountain rather than tree to communicate his thought that 'we are not the weather, we are the mountain' and 'acceptance of the weather that surrounds us is one of the keys for unlocking the process of growth and transformation in our lives.'

Many years ago, after receiving every treatment and drug therapy on offer and after numerous hospital admissions for depression, an enlightened GP referred me to a unit in Guy's Hospital where he had trained. It was ahead of its time, offering talking therapies. After living there for a month, where it felt a privilege to be part of a community of twelve people looking for themselves, I returned home. But very soon the deep darkness returned. It was then, at my own insistence and after initial doubts, that I undertook to attend a period of psychotherapy at Guy's.

One day a week for eighteen months, I travelled from my home in west Wales to Guy's for an hour appointment and back again. Family support was integral and today I marvel at the wonderful person our son has become in spite of living through this period as a young child. The doctors' concern was that what was gained in a session would be lost on the long journey home. The hidden agenda here was that I was not travelling alone but, as with anyone in search of themselves, was accompanied by the one who said 'I am the way, the truth and the light.' This is significant for anyone on such a journey. The more light that was shed on my darkness and the more truth revealed, the more my awareness grew of the divine spirit dwelling within me. At one particular session the therapist suggested 'It is not realistic to expect one person to satisfy all our needs', and on the train journey home my imagination conjured up the presence of Christ on the opposite seat. Awareness flashed momentarily – here was someone who could help me!

Nevertheless after eighteen months of therapy, my depression remained a blanket covering myself and my world, and meaninglessness hung in the very air I breathed.

Then, inexplicably, I awoke one morning to find myself the other side of a decision. I would go to London once more to say 'Goodbye', for the time had come to accept this depression as a part of life: 'Lord, I accept the mystery of being alive. In your own good time you will give me reason for it.' I did so, and from that day to this have never been depressed. Whether this could have happened without the previous months of therapy is unlikely, but that was the day of accepting the person I was and taking responsibility for myself. Saying 'this is how it is' was somehow the alchemy needed for real transformation to begin, which in no way denied both the hard work and healing up to that point.

If accepting darkness makes it not quite so dark, then acceptance of our limitations (having pushed them as far as possible!) opens up the possibility of creativity. The sycamore outside the window accepts its limitation both of space and kind. In school we were taught how each type of tree has a different shape which it grows into. The sycamore will never be an oak, but her transformation will be no less beautiful. Likewise the artist must accept the limitation of his canvas and creativity is born in the way he does this. So we too must live and love from within our personal limitations. Growing older, this becomes something of a hot topic between friends, and accepting certain limitations with ageing seems to be a journey in itself. Blessed by a problem of fatigue at this point in life and having by now befriended what was initially a great diminishment, I find it serves a similar purpose to the monastic idea of enclosure. There are certain activities off limits through weakness rather than choice yet the quality of such times, once accepted, brings with it a depth of experience and an ability (albeit a hard one!) to live by 'being' rather than 'doing'. Within this so-called enclosure, encounter with the Divine brings untold joy.

The struggle is expressed in a poem entitled 'Enclosure', written during a stay on Caldey Island.

In the aftermath of pain
I look out from my enclosure
on the divine beauty blossomed in this place,
the exuberant energy of nature
controlling constant turning tides
and rotating seasons,
basking now in brightness,
generating glory …
and today I am sad
that I cannot join in the dance.

And yet …
It is here in this low-ceiling'd place
where only stillness seeps through the salt-sea-stripped
shutters
that I recognise in the shadows
the spirit of poverty come to greet me.
Beauty herself,
she comes unadorned
and sits easy with one empty-hearted and empty-handed.
Both of us naked,
no offering but ourselves,
she gives me her company
to dance with creation at the still point of its turning,
whilst I remember your promise
in the sweet beauty of your embrace.

So acceptance is creative on many different levels. Not that we should accept our own or another's suffering until we have done all we can to relieve it. My dear mother, now in the last stages of dementia, lives in a small residential home opposite where we live. Never at peace, always anxious or distressed, she still recognises me as a familiar face, sometimes angry with me and the next moment clinging to me. All I can do is to sit with her in it, accepting my powerlessness to relieve her suffering and bring contentment. Acknowledging she is, even now, in God's hands, I utter heart-felt cries for her release.

It will take a life-time of such experiences before being faced with the eventual acceptance of our own death. Whenever that time comes, the icon of ultimate acceptance, Christ crucified, will be there for us whether or not we recognise him. For what made him victor rather than victim was his acceptance of the outcome of the way he had lived, rather than running away from it, which he could have done. It is this very acceptance that is redemptive for those of us coming after him. But maybe more of that another day.

March

GROWTH

New Beginnings

The birds sensed it before we did,
a scarcely noticeable note of joy
amidst the dank darkness of an early March morning;
a lightening of nature's step,
quiet quickening of her heart beat,
with promise of a corner turned
in the fluidity of dance.

The faithful gardener
is first in step,
waiting and watching,
listening for the music,
sensing changes in rhythm,
with sight of crocus and catkin
and the grateful thanks of one well-fed robin.

And something stirs within:
a sweet smell of new beginnings
with scent of opening opportunities
and the chance
to join in the dance
going on outside my window.

Nature is waking up, and today I sense a pulsing of life both around and within the *poustinia*. The limbs of the great chestnut are the first to stretch whilst birds of all species herald a new beginning rising in delighted orchestration of song. Walking down the path this morning, it was possible to hear the garden begin to breathe again, as forget-me-nots and primroses seek to follow snowdrops and daffodils in this jubilant dance of Springtime. It is rejuvenating, too, to make contact with the earth and to be tending the garden again, even if it is only tidying up as yet. Nevertheless, it is good to clear the debris of Winter and make space for new growth.

As sap rises in Nature and in my own deepest self, there comes realisation that any real growth in our human spirit is dependent on awareness and learning to see rather than on accumulating knowledge and virtue. And just as making space in the borders will encourage new growth of plants, so we also need space in order to see clearly. A wise friend, when asked how she would spend her retirement replied, 'guarding the space'. For those of us who have suffered from low self-esteem, it is tempting to fill those spaces with business of any sort, simply to justify being alive or perhaps to avoid meeting our deepest self. But it is difficult to see through clutter and if we are serious about the inward journey, then personal spring-cleaning is important. How often, though, does God himself, disguised as life, make those spaces, through the ordinary things that happen to us? More of that later, but for now it is enough to agree with Marcel Proust that 'the real voyage of discovery consists not in seeking out new landscapes but in having new eyes.' And space to do so is important.

Learning to see, then, is the way of the pilgrim and this does not happen overnight. As Saint Exupéry says in *The Little Prince*, 'the life of the spirit is intermittent. The spirit alternates between total vision and absolute blindness.' Who cannot identify with this? As we set out on the journey, we travel a road edged with lamps and we move from one pool of light to another. Until, that is, our eyes become accustomed to the intermittent darkness and the lights come to an end. Memory recalls one such pool of light whilst travelling on the inter-city. A tragedy had happened in our town where a young child died in an accidental house fire. It affected the whole community and thinking of her on this particular journey, there was a specific and memorable shift of awareness. Instead of imagining myself at the centre of the world, and seeing everything from there, the centre ground shifted to a cross with the child's bereaved family at its foot and me somewhere near the edge of the tableau. It felt like a significant moment, but only much later did I learn that all the great religions teach the need for a different perspective and recognise that the contemplative way of seeing is different from the one which sees everything as personally related.

It has been said that all problems at any level of religious organisations come about because we are all at different stages of growth, and it is true that each of us makes our own individual journey. The road travelled to today's *poustinia* has been long, and I set out on it at a young age, possibly because of attending a church junior school. Already then, I had a sense of encounter and of relating to Christ as friend.

> If Jesus came to my house
> and knocked upon the door,
> I'm sure I'd be more happy
> than I've ever been before.
>
> I'd run downstairs to meet Him,
> the door I'd open wide
> and I would say to Jesus –
> 'Won't you come inside?'

Although not from a church family, this attraction to religion deepened and grew until, during the sixth form, I was ready to be excited by John Robinson's *Honest to God* which exploded on the world. Here for the first time, for people other than academics, God was presented as the ground of our being. Revolutionary at the time, today there is a recognition that self-awareness and God-awareness go hand in hand, although these may well run on parallel paths until the time we realise there is only one path. Before this time, most of us visited a priest for matters of the soul and a psychiatrist for matters of the mind, as psychology was seen as a greater threat than science to Christianity.

At about this point, Harry Williams' *The True Wilderness* floated into vision, and reading this book for the first time was an epiphany moment for me. Here the two worlds of the spiritual and psychiatric became one, and I made the discovery that whatever we complain about, whatever troubles us, is part of the process of our redemption. Only later was I to discover that the Desert Fathers and Mothers already practised this unification, employing in the fourth century the psychology we look upon as new but which was only alienated from religion by Freud. This reintegration is thankfully once more in place.

Fortunate to be able to correspond with Harry Williams while he was a monk at Mirfield, I once asked him whether the appeal of God as father came from an unsatisfactory relationship with a human father. His reply has remained written on my heart ever since: 'God is neither father nor mother but gives us images with which to think of Himself. In this case, he Himself is the picture-slasher and in His own good time He will give you another image with which to think of Him. Do not worry that your dolls have been put in the dustbin; in his own good time, God will give you a pony.' And that is what happened. Over time, God became light, as well as pure presence. Any growth is unsettling because it involves change and takes us out of our comfort zone. Yet being willing to be disturbed is a prerequisite for the pilgrim.

Now that the waves of the spirit have calmed it is possible to see, here in the *poustinia*, that my deepest self and the self of every person is part of the Divine. With such awareness, an earlier love for the Jesuit poet Gerard Manley Hopkins is rekindled, his idea of 'inscape' being that every living thing carries the DNA of the Divine.

The world is charged
with the grandeur of God,
it will flame out, like shining from shook foil;
it gathers to a greatness,
like the ooze of oil crushed

God is not only involved in life, but is that very life itself. He is the in-ness of everything that is and we, individually, are part of this great whole.

Each must find their own way. Traditions can help, as can experiences of others, but I am learning in this little hut that only listening to our own soul will enlighten us, and as Annie Dillard says in *Pilgrim at Tinker Creek* 'the secret of seeing is the pearl of great price.'

April

STILLNESS

AND

LISTENING

The Still Point

To the still point of the world
you bring me,
stripped of illusion,
need-naked before you:
to the foot of your cross
and the gentleness of God
where thought's wings fold in the heart
and future plans melt molten in the fire.

Vulnerable and alone,
hands empty before you,
gathered up in love's gaze
and embraced in your victory.

Earlier this morning the rain fell heavily, like stair-rods, creating a curtain of running water over the open doorway of the *poustinia*. Now suddenly it has stopped, the sun breaks through and stillness settles on the surrounding landscape and on me. Nature holds her breath, the only sound a flap of wings as the heron flies past. The birds begin again to sing, a train is heard in the distance, and raindrops drip from the saturated sycamore onto the roof where I sit. And I am one with it all, held in the stillness and silence of presence.

I am reminded of Elijah's observation that God's voice was not heard in the thunder of the noise of the storm, but in 'the still small voice' that followed. For listening is the bottom line of life in the *poustinia* and stillness its prerequisite. Yet this has not always been so for me and I resonate with Hopkins in his poem, 'Peace', where he longs for and wonders when peace will come to him permanently, rather than as an occasional guest.

> When will you ever, Peace, wild wood dove
> shy wings shut,
> your round me roaming end, and under
> be my boughs?…
>
> And when Peace here does house…
>
> He comes to brood and sit.

It is no accident that the *poustinia* has arrived at the bottom of my garden at this time of life and this point in my journey. Does the Divine always know what we need most and when, I wonder? Such peace and stillness presently experienced within this small shack, though ultimately gift, has been hard won over many years of struggle through dark waters. An old Benedictine friend of mine used to say 'It's all in the struggle' and we all have our stories of such things. It does take a long time before we are able – if ever – to make Jung's mantra our own and believe that 'the contradictions of the circumference are resolved in the still centre'. I have found time and time again that the only answer to severe distress is stillness, if we are able to make it to her door.

Listening has many levels and so much has been written about it that I can only speak with integrity from where it has touched my own life. Although grateful for the therapy received, it is not an essential qualification for listening! However, courage is required to encounter the depths. We all have a dark side as very few of us have been loved well enough, and this shadow needs to be confronted and we must come to terms with it if we are able to hear clearly. In one way or another we need to listen to our life, to our deepest self, to recognise and accept our brokenness. Often, there is a need for another to first listen to our story, to help us to hear it and to see it from another perspective. But why is all this necessary? Because it is in these depths of our own soul that we will eventually hear the voice of the Divine. From a place of deep healing it will tell us how much we are loved and accepted unconditionally, without any need to prove or justify ourselves.

Even so, when stillness does eventually find us, it does not carry a promise that daily life will be peaceful from here on. In an appreciation of Redon's painting 'The Mystical Boat' Sister Wendy Beckett explains: 'The sea is not still, for the one who prays, it heaves and is turbulent. The tossing of the boat is part of the journey. It is the outward stress that makes the surrender of trust vital... The daily living is the choppy sea, but her prayer...is the deep faithful blue of the boat bearing her forward in a power not her own.'

Thrown in at the deep end on a first visit to Tymawr proved to be a great grace. Here was a Community specifically set up for the purpose of listening. Following the Rule of St Benedict (the first word of which is 'listen'), life here is organised specifically around stillness and silence.

Here I learned not only to swim, but to delight in an atmosphere where God could be encountered free from layers of everyday living. The subsequent struggle to integrate such experience into ordinary family life has been on-going and brought with it the company of many soul-friends following the same path; friends of the heart trying to live out contemplation in the market place in the spirit of St Benedict. I should perhaps emphasise that this stillness first encountered at Tymawr, and being brought to fruition at the bottom of my garden, is not the prerogative of convents or the *poustinia*. This silent energy of the Divine is present always at the heart of everything, merely hidden beneath the clutter of our human living. It is ours to access and once we have a taste, or acknowledge our need of it, it is possible to find little deserts everywhere

– while having a coffee in the garden, or kitchen, alone in the car, not to mention walking or fishing from a river bank.

Encouraged and nourished by fellow travellers I have met along the way, life has in many ways been a learning in listening. From the beginning I realised that some time set aside for the purpose each day was necessary, as it is with any relationship we are serious about. Clearing the decks of life also helped, whether this happened naturally through life events such as illness or by a voluntary action. Letting go of clutter leaves freedom and space to listen. In all this, quieting our inward selves is the constant challenge and everyone has their own way of going about it. Abishiktanando (French Benedictine-Indian Swami) is helpful in his book *The Cave of the Heart*: 'Looking for silence is like being on a motor boat racing around the lake looking for a smooth spot where everything is silent and there you are—vroom! Vroom! Vroom! Racing around with increasing anxiety you are never going to get there… All you have to do is throttle back and turn off the key and then there you are. When you start to be receptive, you start to return to your natural state which is very quiet.'

Led in a natural way by a local priest into the practice of Christian meditation (as promoted by World-wide Christian meditation) has proved a very helpful tool. Communicated initially by John Main and continued today under the leadership of Lawrence Freeman (both Benedictine monks), it employs the use of a mantra as an aid for sitting in stillness. Any gardener will say that for growth to endure it must be rooted and this is how I find the practice helps. It offers a way of being grounded in our own centre, through great simplicity.

Of course, all this leads us outwards in listening to others. Of supreme importance, it so often proves to be the greatest thing we can do for someone. However, it is so important that we put time and space between experiencing our own pain and trying to be of help to someone else. True empathy is not a re-telling of our own stories but listening to another's with perhaps heightened compassion. We need time not only to work through our personal pain but to let go of our wounds and step over them into freedom.

So it was that after many years of being free from depression, I began work as a home-help for social services. The job subsequently grew into working as an assistant to the psychiatric social worker on the community mental health team. Past experience proved not only to be the most important qualification but meant that instinctively I was able to listen, because of having previously been listened to. How often was I privileged to witness the beginning of healing of someone who had been able to tell their story, perhaps for the first time! Two days a week I ran a drop-in club for people with mental health problems who lived in the community. The highlight of Summer was a five day stay at the guest house on Caldey Island. For people who never went on holiday, this had all the novelty of going overseas, but the reality is that it was a twenty minute boat trip from Tenby, ten miles away. Together with voluntary helpers we took over the guest house and the island embraced us. A memorable image is of a young, educated schizophrenic standing at the water's edge, holding up a fish he had previously caught and which we were about to cook on a beach fire as the sun was going down. It was this same young man who at one time expressed curiosity about the person of St Benedict, founder of western monasticism. This came out of the blue, because nothing was imposed. I explained that he was a good guy who knew how to live because he wrote of a balanced life of work, prayer and leisure, and that he began his writings with the exhortation 'Listen!' This personable but suffering young man responded: 'Does that mean I should listen to my voices?' Too stunned by his reply to offer any platitudes, I had no answer. Seeing anew that this was the place from where he always began, I could only enfold him in the depth of compassion and listen. Sister Paula (late of Tymawr) used to say, 'Every least encounter is a gesture of His; a means of giving or receiving Christ Himself.' Never have I been more aware of the truth of that.

As I have said, listening is very much part of the raison d'être of the *poustinia*, and I am aware of how much I may have missed which may float downstream to another who waits. Yet without fully understanding, I am aware of the privilege, although retired from working life, of being in a place to listen to peoples' pain and to be open, if only a little, to the wounds of our world. And doing this not alone, but in company with a great crowd of others, holding situations and people, both near and far, in a communal embrace.

Having had visitors for four days and accompanied David to show them our beautiful Pembrokeshire coast, I have failed to listen to my body and am now exhausted.

But no regrets – it was worth it! Perhaps creativity also demands that from time to time we try to push the boundaries.

> Today
> when all strength is sapped away
> and it's not easy
> to see,
> I lie still
> in the cloud
> and wait.
> An empty shell on a deserted beach,
> I wait with the others who wait
> for the sure tide of your love
> which will come
> and sweep us away
> with the wild wonder of your wanting us.

May

RECEIVING

The Sycamore

The sycamore is out fully now
raising its arms
extending leaf-long fingers to receive
the sweetness of Springtime,
and I stand beneath
caught up in her mystery,
arms open wide
to the gentleness of love
saturating my soul.

Rain has fallen in the night, the first after weeks of dry weather and this morning the world is refreshed, renewed and able to breathe again. May is the most beautiful month and walking the path this morning is to witness an explosion that delights. Campions, bluebells and buttercups join coastal-path thrift and low-lying geraniums, while poppies and foxgloves hover waiting in the wings.

Arriving at the *poustinia*, I see Nature laid out before me, waving a welcome with a sea of whiteness. All is gift and all I can do is receive it with gratitude. As the wood pigeon coos 'love you Judy', I am reminded of Alice Summers, the Czech Jew who has just died at the age of one-hundred-and-two. Today it is easy enough to recognise everything as gift, but this amazing woman, a concert pianist incarcerated in Auschwitz for several years, was still able to say 'everything is a present'. This speaks to the heart more than any sermon, shouting out as it does that, whatever life holds, it gives us God. He is that very life itself, in whatever way it touches us, and the real gift is his presence, offered and hidden beneath even the most dreadful circumstances. The treasure is everywhere, offered to us at all times and wherever we may find ourselves. All we have to do is graciously receive it.

Why is this so difficult? A young friend of mine, of great depth and capability, had a dream while studying for the priesthood. A crowd of people surrounded her, carrying bouquets of flowers as gifts. She felt embarrassed and wondered what it meant, until it was suggested she was being asked to receive something. She became distressed, physically shying away from the idea until she was led to see that she was so competent in doing things for God and for others that she was unable to receive what either had to give her. It was a turning point in her life, and my friend went on to become the sort of priest we all wish to know.

But why is it so much easier to do something for somebody, than to let them do something for us? Perhaps because we are brought up to believe 'it is more blessed to give than to receive' and in some circles our worth is valued by what we give in the form of service. Another view is that just to receive from others is a sign either of selfishness or dependence, reminiscent of the behaviour of small children or elderly people. It is counter-cultural to appear passive and it makes us feel diminished, even though it is a quality that makes us more fully human. There is an attitude in our society that we need to be pro-active to be successful or of any worth. In order to build an ego in the first place we do need this, but once we venture beyond these limits to discover our real self it becomes less important. It does require a certain maturity and self-esteem to believe that just being ourselves is the holiest thing we can do.

Perhaps this is why it takes some of us until the second half of life to learn the quality of receiving graciously. Many of us need time before we are able to receive the gifts that grace is waiting to give us. Openness of heart is the pre-requisite for receiving and both time and healing is often required before we can open the closed doors of our inner world. William Holman Hunt's painting 'The Light of the World' springs to mind, for here Christ is standing outside a door where clearly the handle is on the inside. We find many excuses for not being able to open the door, most of which have fear as the underlying cause – the unknown is frightening and it is much safer to remain as we are!

This was brought home to me when I was speaking to a forty-year-old alcoholic, who had been drinking heavily since the age of fifteen. He admitted his life was in shreds, but because he could not remember sobriety it was too frightening and too much of an unknown to even contemplate the journey to it. This applies to less dramatic obstacles to our growth, such as resentment, anger, despair, work, as well as physical illness. We will all need help or healing at some point in our lives if we are to grow into the fully human beings we are meant to be. The word 'healing' is not fashionable today, even though the ministry of Jesus was characterised by the two prongs of preaching and healing. Perhaps the word itself has become too overloaded and we could replace it with 'restoring'.

It was a long time ago, during a bout of severe depression, that the vicar of our town was a great support to me. Often, after an hour of tears and talk, he would lay his hands on my head and pray, always preceding this by saying 'This is simply an act of faith.' The touch helped and with it came a sense of connection to something – love or peace – flowing through his hands. Who knows how much such moments, together with the psychotherapy, helped to unblock doorways for me and transform my life? Sometimes all we need is a willingness to want to be freed.

Although many people will not feel the need for such formal healing, we all need to be ready to respond to whatever way the knock at the door of our hearts presents itself. Boris Pasternak said 'When a moment knocks on the door of your life it is often no louder than the beating of your heart and it is very easy to miss it.' For the most part, healing of blockages to receiving and growing just requires that we be willing and awake to recognise them. Recovery, resurgence, resurrection are all implicit and unbound in Nature, and are discovered too in the depth of the human spirit. I am amazed still today how a dear friend whose husband committed suicide some years ago, has somehow with help come through the trauma. She has said 'yes' to life, continuing to live and love and delight in her grandchildren. Transformation can be the name of the game, if we have the courage to receive it.

So it is that 'receiving' colours the whole of life in the *poustinia*, where it is recognised that the challenge is no longer achievement but making a space to receive the Divine. This is not easy when society rates people on how busy they are: we can fill our life with so many good things and possessions that little room is left for the emptiness God craves to live within us. Indeed, many of our activities are grounded in fear of such emptiness.

In her beautiful book, *Gift from the Sea*, Anne Morrow Lindbergh describes how she began to drop acquisitiveness, to discard and select: 'One cannot collect all the beautiful shells on the beach. One can collect only a few and they are more beautiful if they are a few.'

Nothing is wrong in itself, but this letting go of everything in God's way in order to have space to receive him is an old, rather than new, practice that goes back to the Desert Fathers and Mothers of the fourth century. They left everything to live in the desert so that they could become more fully themselves, without the temptation of putting things between themselves and God. This is the same aestheticism that monastics follow today and mirrors what happens naturally in life when suffering disappointment or failure. Kenosis is the Greek word for the resultant emptiness, and I am now grateful for the kenotic years of depression which had a similar effect. It is the nature of depression to cancel out everything, so there was no need to denounce worldly success, wealth or superfluities because they were stripped away. Similarly, there was no need to imagine or contrive brokenness, the reality being too real. When God becomes the only thing left to trust and even he hides his face, the desert is real. Thus our wounds and those of our world become the spaces for God to enter, and the real challenge is to sustain that space carved out by suffering and not fill it with trivia.

Another side of receiving is practising hospitality of heart towards other people. We are always better able to do this when we have received and accepted our own selves. This deep 'love as yourself' hospitality of which Christ spoke, is very much the sister of *poustinia*. For in order to be really present with another at depth, we need solitude. We are given the people to receive and welcome within our hearts, whether from our own community or on the prayer waves and we hold them, even as we are held, within our consciousness of the Divine presence. Our home has always been a place of welcome for those who visit and who, over the years, have brought many riches of love and friendship. There have been times when there has been an awareness of 'receiving angels' unawares into our home. One of these was an eccentrically dressed old lady who walked around our town carrying a pilgrim staff. Stories often circulated about her unconventional behaviour, but a few of us were given the grace to see beyond the façade:

> The beauty of her face fresh-fired
> by Christ,
> she arrived at our gate
> one drab sunless afternoon,
> an old lady wearing old clothes,
> features shining like a flower peace-petal'd by dew.
> And she brought to our home
> him whom she'd been with;
> steeped still in the silence and sweetness of his love
> she sat by our hearth
> and glowed with his glory,
> his radiance reflected in the ageless wonder of her face.
> And still, heart speaks to heart,
> though she's no longer with us,
> whilst her staff stands – bequeathed – in the corner of
> the room,
> symbol of stillness
> pattern of pilgrimage
> journey continuing to the place she has gone.

June

JOY AND LAUGHTER

MIDSUMMER MORNING

Midsummer morning after a night of
torrential rain
and the Pembrokeshire lanes lie freshly
laundered,
held in a stillness
like the aftermath of pain.
The foxgloves are brighter today,
newly painted in the morning mist;
and joy shouts from the banks of the way –
still wet with tears,
but sheltered by the overhanging branches
of your care.

It is high Summer and the garden aflame with beauty. Walking the path this morning, after a week away, is to witness yet more surprises she has in store. Poppies and foxgloves, now in full-flowering wonder, accompany campanula and the first of the roses to reflect the summer face of the Divine here in the garden. The big surprises are the large white daises in the meadow, seeded somehow from the roadside. They welcome me on my way, and when I arrive at the *poustinia* birds sing and swoop delightedly. An occasional 'plop' from the stream speaks of small trout on their way up river, saluted by comfrey overflowing the banks. God says 'Enjoy my world', and all of Nature joins in the chorus.

The *poustinia* and the garden are teaching me about joy. There are times here when an awareness of being loved floods my whole being. Sometimes it is only a moment but, however long, awareness soon arrives that these times cannot be orchestrated, but only received. All is gift. I believe joy has a glow, unlike the fire of happiness, a deep-down knowing that all is well, that underneath everything that happens is promise of resurrection. Perhaps it has something to do with letting go of the story of me and entering the eternal now.

Today there is news that two unlikely literary collaborators, the Dalai Lama and Archbishop Tutu, are to explore together this topic of joy and publish it in a joint work. The two Nobel Peace laureates are to meet in Dharamsala for five days and spend time 'in deep dialogue and playful laughter' as they share their experience of how to find joy in the face of life's challenges. 'The ultimate source of happiness is within us' said the Dalai Lama, 'not money, not power, nor status, which fail to bring inner peace. Outward attainment will not bring real inner joyfulness; we must look inside.' Tutu said, 'Sometimes life can be challenging and we can feel lost, but the seeds of joy are born inside each of us.'

Is it a Welsh characteristic that many of us have been more at home in darkness that light? The influence of those brooding mountains and the weather and the male voice choirs all contribute with the sonorous sound of Dylan Thomas to finding depth in darkness rather than light. When our granddaughter spent a year with her father in Key West she spoke of feeling different from the Florida girls who, living in permanent sunshine, had a much lighter attitude to life. In my own experience, real joy, which is not the same as feeling happy, is arrived at through a dark tunnel and is always a surprise. A Spring morning of many years ago is still vivid. Coming out of a deep depression, the dark cloud suddenly lifted to reveal the world of Nature in startling colours accompanied by the most melodic sounds. Such joy is deep, but light too, and involves play. We recognise it in the young of every species, especially in children and lambs.

Joy is also what makes old people young again. In the last stages of dementia, my mother is more anguished than happy. Most days I sit with her for a while in her dark place, just hoping it may help. Then, one day, the little home where she lives enrolled an Elvis look-alike for entertainment. As soon as the music began it was a light-bulb moment and my mother became young again, her face shining with the delight of a child. We even had her up and dancing! This was something we repeated for her several times and on each occasion the music had the same effect. Such an experience of joy has a simplicity that we possess as children but often forget. It lies the other side of complicatedness and I cannot think of it without remembering Sister Cara, late of the Tymawr Community. Familiar with the dark places of human experience, she yet embodied an instinctive familiarity with joy. I think of her dancing with the whole of herself on a local beach when she came to visit, and of being concerned for her safety as she skipped like a child along the narrow coastal paths.

Caldey Island (home to a Community of Cistercian monks) is very vivid in the *poustinia* today. Yesterday, on a cloudless day without a breath of wind, a boat-load of us travelled across the water from Tenby to the funeral of Fr Stephen, a monk of the Community. We went to give thanks for a well-loved friend and the life he had lived. The island sparkled like a jewel in celebration of his wisdom and transparency. Fr Stephen was one of the longest serving members of the Community and in his homily Abbot Daniel spoke lovingly of this humble monk, who looked after the practical business of the island for thirty years. He spoke of how, in his final years, having searched for the meaning of life, Fr Stephen concluded it was hidden somewhere within the lightness of pure laughter. I was reminded of a friend I have previously mentioned

– Harry Williams, himself a monk. In his book *Tensions*, where he wrote of life's complexities, he too reached the conclusion that the answer to the universe lay in laughter. He says that, in the sort of laughter where we can see the funny side of things and especially of ourselves, we sit light to our own person; this he sees as the purist form of our response to God.

Six small trout swim past the window, while squirrels play on a neighbouring branch. How often we forget that God wants us to be happy and longs for us to receive his joy!

July

JESUS

THE UNDERGROUND SPRING

You are the underground spring
that flows through the moments of my day,
unseen beneath the surface of each least encounter,
giving glory to little things
through the current of your love.
But here in the stillness of this solitary place
you burst from beneath
to rise shimmering in sunlight –
torrent of tenderness fresh-flowering the desert,
silent stream of love flooding the earth.

The school holidays have just begun and the population of Pembrokeshire has increased three-fold. All the visitors need is sunshine, but it is raining day after day. The garden is sodden but resilient, with many cottage garden plants like poppies 'going over', and the main job being to continue dead-heading roses and geraniums. It is time for the annuals to take centre stage and cosmos and antirrhinums give splendid colour to the garden, while one of my favourite plants, sea-holly, blooms amongst the pebbles, reminiscent of the sand dunes on Caldey. The sweetest smells come from an old fashioned Queen Victoria rose mingling with the mock orange and honeysuckle. Picking sweet peas daily is a delight unaffected by the unseasonal weather.

From the *poustinia* today, I look out on a world refreshed by rain and lit by momentary sunshine into the summer face of the Divine. It is the gaze of Christ that imagination reveals looking back at me. He has been with me from the beginning, a constant guide and companion on this long journey in search of peace, but I have never looked into his face until now. As I do, I find there such depth which touches the deepest part of myself, confronting me with the question, 'Who do you say that I am?' It is both an invitation and challenge to look closer and discover more about him. This will involve taking the search beyond the heart-space of the *poustinia* to the world of investigation through reading, then bringing any treasure discovered back here to integrate into experience and enrich our relationship. Many of us were taught about Jesus rather than encouraged to relate to him. Maybe it is something to do with this that his name has such a bad press today, being seen either as illusionary or irrelevant. My task will be to search for the real Jesus in the same way that old masters are renovated, that is by careful removal of layers of grime accumulated over the years. The hope is that the original can then be witnessed in something of its vividness and vitality. It will be a journey led by Christ in search of himself.

Naturally, the real work of exploration has been done by theologians who have devoted their lives to finding the real Jesus, and mine is no more than to consider the fruits of their research. Nevertheless, it requires some courage and a willingness to be disturbed, to be led from my comfort zone into a more truthful and exciting dimension. Richard Rohr has said 'God and truth never just fall into our lap but are only given as gifts to those who really want them and deserve them.' More prosaically, Elizabeth Gilbert in *Eat, Pray, Love* says '… if man never evolved in this exploration of the Divine a lot of us would still be worshipping golden Egyptian statues of cats.' Setting out on this journey, an old song rises from the deep:

> Getting to know you
> getting to know all about you,
> getting to like you
> getting to hope you like me …

For some time I have been aware of a developing consciousness of the Divine happening across the world and now there is a sense of joining a stream of thought and experience that is already going on, and which proclaims Jesus is met in the centre of ourselves, where recognition brings transformation of life. This allows growth to happen, breaking through our small egotistical self into the larger self, of the spirit, that Jesus refers to as the Kingdom of God. I am reassured that it is not necessary to be a scholar or live in a monastery to become part of this stream, which is for everyone who searches for depth below the surface of life. Daniel O'Leary, in one of his *Tablet* articles affirms, 'the reality of everything is only beginning to be understood'.

Perhaps this is the place to say that I speak here of a personal response to that reality and many deeply spiritual people may find they disagree with, or are disturbed by what follows in this chapter. If so, they should feel free to follow their own drumbeat, while I am mindful of Sister Jeanne, late of Tymawr, who used to say 'All we can do is to follow the light we have been given and pray for more light.' That light, with understanding, so often comes in unexpected ways, just as the right book amazingly falls into our hands when needed.

That book today is *Wisdom Jesus*, by Cynthia Bourgeault, an Episcopal priest, teacher and retreat leader. Here, she encourages us to put aside what we think we know about Jesus and approach the gospels as though for the first time. Going back to original sources and texts, cleaning our image of him, she presents Jesus as emerging from the ancient wisdom tradition of the Near East, which was first encountered by Israel during exile in Babylon. She sees one of the losses of the Christian West as being our lack of awareness of this first title given to Jesus by his followers. He was a wisdom master because his parables and sayings helped people wake up to the whole of themselves. His was wisdom of the heart, which allows life to be a mystery, whilst trusting it is of divine origin.

We recognise the Desert Mothers and Fathers of the fourth century as the first official Christian wisdom school, with their stories and sayings that speak directly to our centre. For example, 'Abba Lot went to see Abba Joseph and said to him, "Abba as far as I can, I say my little office, I fast a little, I pray and meditate, I live in peace. What else can I do?" Then the old man stood up and stretched his hands towards heaven; his fingers became like ten lamps of fire and he said to him, "If you will, you can become all flame".' It was this wisdom that Jesus taught: the Kingdom of heaven is within and around you, presenting a state of non-dual consciousness with no separation between God and humanity. 'I and the Father are one', suggests Cynthia Bourgeault, 'was not meant exclusively but was to be shared by everyone'.

Following this path with an open mind and heart, I can see that a great deal of spirituality speaks of our struggle towards oneness with the Divine, together with the belief that it cannot be realised in this life. But now I learn that, as a teacher of the path of inner transformation, Jesus tells us we are already one with God and our only problem is that we are blind and cannot see it! Likewise, his charge to 'Love your neighbour as yourself' tells us that, as well as being united with the Divine, we are one with each other. Food for thought to take back to the *poustinia*.

Going further, peeling more layers off the picture of Jesus, I see that he surprised people by saying that the Kingdom of God had already come. This was counter-intuitive to the people of Israel who were waiting to be released from slavery and established in their own land by a powerful leader. What Jesus proclaims is completely new! He says God is the inner core of everything, and our religion is not about rules and believing right things, but about relationship. However, Cynthia Bourgeault believes that 'with Augustine's theory of original sin in the fifth century, Jesus was repositioned from a wisdom teacher to a mediator, and the spiritual journey reframed from a quest for divinization to a rescue operation'.

I have found this such an important discovery it takes time to get my head around it, together with acceptance of the fact that for so long we have been presented with a distorted view of Jesus. The journey continues! Having been nurtured by Cistercian monastic Communities, knelt at their altars and delighted in the presence of God amongst them, I can verify the validity of an aesthetic way of life. However, I now discover that this is not the only, or even preferred way to God. The Jesus I am now meeting puts up no barriers to protect his life with God; rather he 'gives it all away' in a kenotic way of living, relying on God to keep on giving. With abundant generosity and giving of self, everything is embraced but, importantly, nothing is clung to either.

Back in the *poustinia* this morning comes realisation that, while my search for Jesus is becoming more intensive through thinking and reading, his presence here is more palpable than ever. It is confirmation to me to continue as light is beginning to be shed on the end of his life. This is the part that especially asks for courage because what is being hinted at does not conform to any teaching previously received. Forty years ago I asked the question, 'Why was it necessary for Jesus to die?', and down through the years I have never received a satisfactory explanation. Until now, that is, when I can see that the answer is simply that it was not necessary – at least not in the way of appeasing an angry God so that sins could be forgiven. Now I begin to see Jesus' death as the result rather than the meaning of his life and learn that, looking back on that life, the early Christians needed to find a reason for the awful circumstances of the crucifixion.

Jose Pagola, in his amazing work *Jesus – an Historical Approximation* says, 'He (Jesus) saw no significance or meaning in his death, only that the reign of God would come to fullness after his death.' I can see now that with Jesus proclaiming his message for the leaders of Israel as well as the common people, he would have been a threat to them. His eventual death then is less surprising than inevitable. What is extraordinary is that he could have got out of it by disclaiming his message but instead remained faithful to the deepest part of himself. A bridge between realms, Jesus came to be with us rather than save us, giving his life and death to see us through. Don Macgregor, author of *Blue Sky God*, explained this well during an inspiring retreat at St Non's on the cliffs outside St David's. He spoke of Jesus being unique because 'he fulfilled the potential of humanity to become Divine.

This allowed him to break through barriers, like death, so the rest of us could follow, hanging on to his coat tails'. Perhaps, it seems to me, this is 'saving us' but in a different way than we were previously taught. Don went on to say that when we pray we touch into this Christ-energy: dying to the small self and rising with Christ is the way of transformation. A living parable then, where we see the ultimate revelation of God in a person!

This takes me back to biblical studies in former days, and the thrill of discovering the Old Testament as a drama, where God took a small nation, Israel, and through the events of their history revealed himself to them. Gradually, over two thousand years, with the help of prophets to interpret their history, the people learned more of what Yahweh, their God was like. Finally, the only way of complete disclosure, was God in human form. So Jesus did not arrive out of nowhere, nor did he come to accomplish, but to reveal. It is significant that his last words were 'It is finished', meaning not only his own life but the whole revelation of God throughout the history of Israel.

An old missionary with a shining face visited our church when I was younger. I confided to him: 'My problem is I get excited about all this.' 'My dear', he said, 'I still get excited.' And today it is possible to appreciate that this is how contact with Jesus affects people, both during his earthly life, and in the present. In the peace and seclusion of the *poustinia*, this same Jesus whose resurrection pulled his friends out of despair, continues to become vivid. In his company I am embraced and fulfilled, recognising him now as part of my deepest self as well as surrounding nature and our whole world. Being here in the womb of nature daily throughout the year, it is possible to experience the cycle of death and rebirth going on outside as well as recognising it on a personal level.

> I saw my Lord with my heart's eye
> and said, 'Who are thou, Lord?'
> Thyself', he replied.
>
> Sufi poet

August

PRAYER

EMPTY-HANDED BEFORE YOU

Some days I have nothing to offer you
but my willingness to be here,
empty-handed before you
with no strength to reach out,
and the ceiling so low
there is no room for anything
except yourself
and the pain.
Then they hang in my heart
as I hang
in this moment,
people given
to share with you.

Just for today, Lord,
accept my weakness
as my prayer
for them.

I t seems as if each season comes earlier these days. Although still August, there is a sense of cooling in Nature, and, as I make my way to the *poustinia*, I sense a hint of Autumn in the air. Already the colours of the garden are changing from vibrant reds and orange to the more muted blues and purple of delphiniums and loosestrife. A mist hangs over the stream, and in the stillness Nature seems to hold her breath, aware of the fall in energy soon to come, when sap will return to the roots even during her time of greatest fruition.

Today it is thoughts on prayer which rise into my consciousness. Raison d'être and life-blood of the *poustinia* in every season, prayer is as difficult to articulate as my life lived with David, and this is perhaps a happy analogy. Basic similarities come to mind as both relationships were initiated by attraction and built on the bed-rock of love. Moreover there is only one love, and the love with which I love my husband is the same that flows between God and myself. Love is difficult to speak of and perhaps it is only poetry that gets close, so anything expressed here will be no more than a finger pointing at the moon. One thing that can be said, however, is that relationships of any kind do not stand still and, with commitment on both sides, will develop and deepen over time. At this point in life, having passed through times of turbulence and stress, David and I are happy to be in each other's company, often in silence. Likewise, prayer has become a simple 'being with' the Divine, with silence largely the language of communication.

In spite of this, on a low-energy day with Nature reflecting my own lack of strength, it feels as though I have little to bring to this relationship except a willingness to be here. It is then I am reminded of the words of St Paul: 'Three times I asked the Lord to take this thing from me. But he said to me, "My strength is sufficient for you, for my power is made perfect in weakness".' Here I dimly perceive that fatigue or any other debility or diminishment can, when accepted, become a help rather than hindrance in the life of prayer. With less of self to get in the way, the continuous prayer of Christ for our world is freer to flow through us. So it is that the frustration and debility of a late-onset condition can be turned on its head and transformed into a vehicle of grace.

'Being there' is important in all love-making, involving an open offering of self in trust to another. It is exciting to discover that the rule of the lay Northumbria Community involves Availability and Vulnerability, and I am affirmed by this. Thinking of the second of these qualities leads on to acknowledging the vulnerability of God, which is a shattering insight, but without which there can be no authentic relationship. The idea of the Divine so close-up and personal initially blows the mind because it speaks of reciprocity between Christ and the soul, an insight that can only be received with wonder. There comes to mind the sculpture outside Chester Cathedral of Jesus giving a drink to the woman at the well, whilst she reciprocates by doing the same for him.

The work is so beautiful and rounded, portraying both figures as part of the same whole. It also reminds me of the story of the old Curé d'Ars who, when asked what he did all the hours he was seated in front of the altar, replied 'I look at Him and He looks at me, and we tell each other we love each other'.

All the experiences and happenings of life have resulted in barriers being broken down between me and others, and between me and the Divine, showing we are all one within the oneness of God. So it is that I begin to see all prayer as intercession, whether we are consciously holding a person or situation in mind, or simply just being in the presence of God. We are part of something greater than ourselves and whatever we do affects the whole, whether we are aware of it or not. Many years ago I felt unable to say the Jesus Prayer ('Lord Jesus Christ have mercy on me'), until I learnt from an Orthodox priest that 'me' was said consciously as part of the whole world. So it is that belief flowers, with the illustration of a butterfly flapping its wings in the Amazon affecting events in down-town New York.

Awareness of this interconnectedness comes to some of us after many years of struggle and to others in a flash of recognition. From its first arrival I have been aware that this gift of the *poustinia* at the bottom of the garden is not purely for my own well-being and happiness. Now I can see that because each of us is part of the whole, the peace of any one of us can influence our planet for good as much as any deed of altruism. Only now in retirement has the constant struggle between action and contemplation resolved itself, and the scales have tipped in my case towards life in the *poustinia*. Service in prayer rather than active involvement is generally a natural development with age, for which I am grateful.

At the time of writing, a very disturbing video has been broadcast on Channel Four showing small children being trained by ISIS extremists in violence. They were instructed to practise by chopping off the heads of teddy bears, while the caption reads: 'this is our future'. Surely this is a call for those who take prayer seriously to join hands around the world, for the sake of our world.

It is important we remember that, to be effective, what we call prayer will always be the prayer of Christ flowing through us. For the most part, we allow this to flow wherever he wills and without any knowledge of where that may be. One of the monks on Caldey Island tells a beautiful tale of when he was a novice and the Abbot called him after supper to walk with him in the dark up to the lighthouse. Once there, the wise old monk shared his vision: 'That light saves the lives of countless people it does not know exists, and its only responsibility is to keep the glass clean.'

Nevertheless, it is also true that from time to time we are personally given specific people and situations to hold in prayer. Then we have the privilege of standing before God for the sake of another for whom we are aware. Sometimes, especially with family and friends, it can be very difficult to trust that all that is happening is within the love of God and that all will be well. I am learning that earnest intercession is mostly about being still, in the centre of a situation, handing it over and trying not to interfere by a desire to fix things. Prayer then becomes holding the tension. We all want life to be good and turn out well for those we love, but sometimes we can only entrust them to God when we are unable to see a good outcome. It is at these times that we can only believe we are seeing the wrong side of a tapestry being created.

Some situations do not have a happy resolution in our eyes, and then we must remain in prayer there, but if asked to do so we will find we are not carrying the pain alone. In the words of John Main, founder of World Wide Christian Meditation: 'The central message of the New Testament is that there is really only one prayer and that is the prayer of Christ. It is a prayer that continues in our hearts day and night. It is the stream of love that flows constantly between Jesus and the Father. It is the Holy Spirit and we have to allow this prayer to become our prayer.'

I have had the privilege of knowing just a few people whose lives have become so transparent that it can be said they themselves are a prayer. Perhaps this is unrealistic for us more ordinary mortals, but the adventure that is prayer is offered to every one of us, finding expression in our differing circumstances and personalities. And if we do accept this invitation, which will not seem to let us go, then over the years we may eventually reach the point where we can say with Laurence Freeman (of present day WWCM): 'Only after time do we see that the path we chose was actually the path we were chosen for.'

September

ORDINARY TIME

Each Day A Feast Day

The west wind calls round the steepled church
through stained glass faces
of saints frozen in sanctity,
but today there is escape
from the dusty pews and wall'd-in piety
to follow Deiniol through fresh-furnished fields
and sit silent with Govan
by this wild wonder of a sea.

Here where Celtic saints
see the whole world as sacred,
earth touches heaven
in the miracle of everyday;
each day is a feast day,
every duty a sacrament,
and the mundane transformed
by the wonder of your love for us.

The business people of our town agree that the day the children return to school after the summer holidays has the effect of closing a door for the local community. From one day to the next the influx of visitors disappears, car parks are emptied, familiar faces once again recognised in the main street, and the atmosphere changes completely. Most of us who welcome people at the beginning of the season are not too sad to see them go again and the place return to itself and its soul. It is essentially a Celtic heart that beats beneath the surface of this part of west Wales and, dating back centuries, it carries treasures from the spirituality of that time that are very relevant to our lives today.

The Celtic mind was characterised by a marriage of the everyday and the eternal. With no distinction between the secular and the sacred, the Celtic people found the presence of the Divine within their ordinary everyday lives. Instinctively, work and prayer were not separated for them, and we recognise this vision in the many songs and rituals handed down:

> Bless, O God, my little cow,
> Bless, O God, my desire,
> Bless though my partnership
> And the milking of my hands, O God.*

*from *Carmina Gadelica*: prayers, poems and songs from the Gaelic oral tradition of the Highlands and Islands of Scotland collected by Alexander Carmichael and first published in 1900.

We have been fortunate in this part of the world to have had teachers to excite interest in Celtic spirituality, and to encourage us to breathe it into our own lives. Hence my poem was only written relatively recently, and the vision of the extraordinary hidden within the ordinary colours any future search for the Divine.

Yet, as a young student, there was a real fear of being ordinary. Expectations were great: to succeed and fly further than the environment we were brought up in. The first generation to reach university from families whose parents never had the opportunity, this was true for many of us. I recall passing towns of terraced houses on the train journey home through south Wales, and articulating to myself, 'I could never live in such an ordinary place with nothing happening!' Today, it is possible to see a smile on the metaphorical face of the Divine! For here I am, at the other end of life, living in a crescent of cottages, having found the treasure of my heart at the bottom of the garden! How did this transformation happen? Life happened – ordinary, unexpected events common to every person, accompanied by the great blessing of love on every level, together with being nurtured in seeing what goes on beneath the surface of life. It is the experience of many, a story of growing through suffering to resurrection and transformation. A story of redemption that is happening in all those terraced houses I had looked at so disdainfully.

Everyone has a story to tell and happy are we if we find someone to share its telling. These stories are filled with events, relationships, tears and joys, mostly unremarkable from the outside, all part of the fabric of human living. If only we could see what is happening during a very ordinary day, we would not be able to stop from dancing! I believe that to discover the extraordinary within the ordinary is life's greatest gift. We may only catch glimpses here and there of this great mystery of which we are part, but it is enough to keep us awake and appreciative of everyday life as 'the simplest and most effective way to sanctity'. (Thomas Merton)

Brother Laurence, a cook from a Carmelite monastery living in seventeenth century France, has been a life-long inspiration and friend. In his little book *The Practice of the Presence of God*, he tells how his times of prayer were no different from other times. He was aware of God's presence as much in the kitchen as in the chapel: 'The time of business does not with me differ from the time of prayer. In the noise and clutter of my kitchen I posses God in as great tranquillity as if I were upon my knees at the Blessed Supper.' His was a way of walking with God continually, in his heart rather than his head, and this way of living is available to any one of us.

Another influence has been Jean-Pierre de Caussade, a Jesuit priest who lived in the eighteenth century. His treatise, *The Sacrament of the Present Moment,* has also been a loyal friend over the years. He speaks of each moment as a gift of God himself: '… there is not a moment in which God does not present himself under cover of some pain, consolation or duty'. So we see that the present moment, whatever it brings, is an 'ambassador for God' and a source of sanctity hidden in the shadows of our daily life. The treasure is everywhere, offered to us at all times, wherever we may be. While working for social services, I used to visit a drop-out caravan site, for people with nowhere else to go. There I met a Cockney rogue called Charlie and witnessed his divine DNA exposed.

The last hold before homelessness,
yet here's where I find you
who never ceases to surprise,
the Jester of Calvary,
who turns the world upside down!
The spirit of Christ
rising resilient
as charged by the chuckle of a toothless cockney rascal,
heaven's laughter is loosed
by this beggar of grace.

As activities and the excitement of summer visitors gives way to ordinary time, I begin to think of 'putting the garden to bed' for the winter. This will involve work in each border: cutting back, dividing perennials like the pink ground geraniums and planting bulbs of daffodils and tulips for next Spring. Meanwhile, I am still picking Michaelmas daises, verbena and cosmos, while thinking of taking the red geraniums under the veranda to shelter from frost. The more tidying done now the easier it will be in the Spring, but some seeds will be left for the birds which have begun coming to the feeders again. Studying each border with thoughts for next year, I take a little time to be grateful for the wonder of the garden this year. And I am part of it! Its soul feeds mine as I tend to its needs, and it keeps me grounded in the sanctity of the present moment. I sense here the value of standing still and going deeper in 'the beauty of one good place' (Thomas Merton).

October

DIMINISHMENT

THE FIRST CHILL

How different it all is when Summer goes
and the first chill of Autumn
cools the ardour of those heady love-long days;
passion past spending,
your features fade into the mellowing mist
and silence settles
on the flaming fire of our love.

And yet …
glowing embers
reflect
the richness of the cooling earth
and there is promise
in the bulging branch –
with hint of other passion yet to come.
The burnish'd beauty of your going
holds a promise and a pain that's all its own.

R eturning from a week away, I find that Autumn has made its mark. After days of wild wind and rain, the ash tree by the side of the *poustinia* stands almost naked, her few remaining leaves falling into the risen waters of the stream. Meanwhile, sheltered in the nature reserve opposite, the oaks and sycamores are still dressed in autumn colours and stand bejewelled in the weakening sun. The year has turned and all we can do is go with it. Autumn is an in-between time, a buffer between Summer (if we are lucky!) and the bareness of Winter, giving us time in temperate climates to adjust to the changes of season. Leaves do not generally fall overnight, the process taking several weeks or even more than a month in some areas, delighting us with golden colour as the days shorten. This is speeded-up on our exposed western coast, where salt from the sea burns the leaves which fall prematurely. But the garden is still bright with colour, thanks to the verbena and phlox and late-planted cosmos. Marigolds too still flower to brighten the darkest spot, and I shall leave these to continue giving pleasure, before cutting back for Winter.

Once again this background of the natural world which surrounds the *poustinia* offers a parable that mirrors our own lives. In Nature, Autumn is accepted as a natural part of the life cycle, yet somehow we fail to recognise ourselves as part of the same process, recoiling at any hint of diminishment or lessening of faculties and physical strength. Most of us do not go straight from summertime to the winter of our lives; we would hardly be able to bare it. A few have no choice and need our support as they come to terms with whatever may have happened to them. Some will have suffered from life-changing sickness, disability or tragedy, but for the most part the rest of us will experience a period in our lives which gives us time to learn to relinquish and let go of much we may have accumulated.

An important and meaningful, if painful time, this stage of life comes to us in different ways and various guises. Perhaps working life has come to an end and our sense of importance is wavering, or our family has grown up and we are no longer needed in the way we were. Age, sickness or grief may touch us personally, while our bodies may not allow us to do all the things we used to do. And we are afraid, so we run from the vulnerability and emptiness that could become a reality. For people who come to this hour without much experience of loss it can be an especially difficult time. Yet few arrive here without disappointment of one sort or another, and now it is possible to see the value of such past experiences in preparing us for greater loss to come.

We cope with the diminishment of age in various ways and with differing degrees of acceptance. Society itself offers no positive message for the slowing-up process and mostly we can see no meaning in our situation. Problems with knees, hips and lack of energy, not to mention diseases like cancer, are seen as miserable and often avoidable if only we were to practise keeping fit. And yet, if I believe that God is in everything going on, I must accept that my slower progress to the *poustinia* because of an aching hip is within his love and purpose. If God is life itself, then he is in the most miserable of situations and experiences, albeit in our own corner, wanting what is best for us. Our problem is that we cannot see the whole picture of what is in the process of being created.

> It isn't easy being made,
> submitting
> to the melting down and hammering into shape,
> feeling only the pain
> without knowing the beauty.
> Only stillness helps,
> relaxing battered bodies and half-finished creations
> into the sure hands of the craftsman,
> and trusting
> that the chalice he has chosen to create
> will prove fit for the wine of his presence.

I would like to suggest that experiences of diminishment through natural events and circumstances are integrated into life for our benefit, and what appears a downward spiral is, in fact, growth into another dimension. Greatly helped by Richard Rohr (again!) at this point, I find he explains the idea so succinctly it justifies the following quote: 'The path of descent is the path of transformation. Darkness, failure, death and woundedness are our primary teachers rather than ideas and doctoring.' He reminds us that 'in all spiritual literature of the world, we need to "lose" something to go forward. This takes us out of the egocentricness of our comfort zone, breaks down the false self, and opens us up to love'(from *Falling Upwards*).

Yet rarely is this as simple as just saying it, and for the majority of us it entails a life-long learning in awareness. It would have been so good and certainly less painful to have had this vision at twenty, when moving from university to a psychiatric ward felt like the end of the world. But the very nature of this descent or diminishment demands we are blind to what is really happening. If this were not so, if we were aware that it was a step up rather than down, somehow it would cease to work – our ego would become even more inflated! Jung too has said 'Where you stumble and fall there you find pure gold.'

And today I find it is possible to be grateful for this downward movement so early in life and for the subsequent years of struggle with depression. 'How can you be thankful for so much pain and trauma?', I hear you ask. Because this was the cauldron in which my relationship with the Divine was forged. When a person has been through the fire, it can be said that what emerges is real. Superfluities and unnecessary distractions are stripped away, leaving the ensuing emptiness in the person as entry point for the Divine, and ready to receive him.

Of course it is not mandatory to suffer before entering a relationship with God – it simply provides a wonderful kick-start and short-cut. Perhaps need though is the one thing necessary, and this is the very thing we run from. Ours is a story of redemption: the same plot for all of us, even when we are unaware of it. It is about transformation and creating something good out of what seems to be of little positive value. Diminishment of any sort is part of this process, perhaps especially when all we can do is accept and hang on, live it from within, and trust. A poster on a young friend's wall reads, 'It is not what is going to become of us, but what we are going to become.'

This way of diminishment is, of course, the way of the cross, the way Jesus came to show us by joining with us and forging a path to follow. He taught that his process downward leads from death to resurrection, for us as for himself. Yet this message is as counter-intuitive today as it was two thousand years ago. There is no glory in diminishment, neither do we like the look of it. Whatever is happening on a positive level is hidden from the eyes of the sufferer and the one who witnesses. Yet, by denying pain and avoiding falling, many who started out on the journey stop themselves from continuing it. Over the last few years we have accompanied my mother on a downward spiral of dementia, where all the senses rebel against the process taking place. Whenever she is agitated and in deep distress, then it is very difficult – impossible rather –to see anything good, let alone divine, in her situation. It is at this point, as love grows (we have never been so close before) and as compassion is stretched and strengthened, that only trust remains.

> The shaft is bottomless;
> hurtling
> from life and from loves,
> helpless
> in the thickening, tumbling-down darkness,
> the final foothold of hope – far-flung.
> Where are you Lord?

Only trust echoes back,
Only trust is given;
God in hell
Christ in the well
of the garden
of Everyman.

Returning this morning to the *poustinia*, I become aware that Nature's struggle is over and calm has settled on her nakedness. She has accepted her dying and the few remaining leaves fall as prayers into the stream, which will carry them to the ocean and the waiting heart of God.

November

DARKNESS

Winter days of your absence
hidden from the sun,
when the world becomes dark
without touch of your smile;
then I stand with the trees
together against the wind
tears frozen on our face,
arms stretched toward heaven,
longing
for warmth,
and the Spring of your return.

The moon is still up as I walk the path this morning. The river is flowing freely, and again I think of the tide that goes in and out twice daily, pulled by the force of the moon. As the sky lightens, I am struck by this backcloth of Nature where night comes every twenty-four hours and there is nothing we can do about it! Darkness will come too at some time in life to each individual in the guise of ordinary events and losses; relationships going wrong, security being threatened, loneliness, fear, tragedy or sickness. A deeper suffering than any diminishment we may have previously experienced, this darkness cuts deeper, into the very bones, sinews and heart of the person we are.

A weaver friend has a plaque on the wall of his workshop: 'The dark threads are as needful as the threads of gold and silver in the pattern he has planned'! Although we understand this in the context of creating cloth, it is hard to give darkness the same value as light in our lives, and we will do absolutely anything to escape it. This is necessary in the sense that we should do anything we can to alleviate suffering both for ourselves and others. However, it is what we are then left with that is important. Perhaps we only have the right to speak from personal experience as we cannot fully appreciate the depth of another's pain until we have 'walked for a day in their moccasins'. Speaking from within that personal place,

I feel that darkness has been a vehicle for my journey to awareness of the Divine. With a severe breakdown the inner self is dismantled, resulting in loss of any sense of identity beneath a blanket of bewilderment and meaninglessness. Only in retrospect is it possible to appreciate the gradual transformative healing process that has occurred. Fortunate in having hands to hold on to, and surrounded by love even without knowing it, distress often expressed itself in a sense of the absence of God. 'Can God get through depression and other mental health problems?' was a frequent question I asked of anyone who might possibly have an answer. It was thus, overtaken by need, that I arrived at Tymawr, with long hair, copious tears and several packets of cigarettes! Here, through the love of the Community, came the experience of 'underneath are the everlasting arms'. That place, with its people, would subsequently become a constant loving companion on a long journey in search of peace.

Part of the darkness, and I suspect part of all deep suffering, was a sense of isolation, being outside places, people and life in general. The act of suicide has been described as a person walking into the sea, unable to hear the cries of family and friends urging him or her back to life. One of the many graces of today and of time spent in the *poustinia* is the realisation that there is no isolation, however real that may feel. Just as there is only one love flowing from the Divine, so there is only one suffering in which we all share, where we are united and caught up together in Christ. It was in the darkness that trust grew:

> And what else is there to do
> when led through unknown country
> at night
> by a guide who goes his own way,
> keeping his thoughts to himself?
> What else, but to put yourself in his hands?

Fortunate in being loved from an early age, trust came more easily for me than for some people with unhappy experiences. A particular session of psycho-drama remains vivid. The leader drew an imaginary line of trust from one corner of the room to the other, representing 0-100%, and asked us to stand where we thought we were. I alone was at around 80%, while everyone else stood at the bottom end. Opportunity came to flex the muscles of trust on another occasion. After being in hospital for a while, I knew it was time to leave but was afraid. One night, I was given grace to entrust at a deep level the whole of myself and my future into Divine hands.

> Past all points of no return,
> with no bird in the hand
> should the two in the bush get away,
> I stake my life on your promise
> and, taking your hand,
> plunge headlong into the all-embracing darkness.

The next day I asked to leave. Healing had begun and I was aware of an infinitesimal strength within that was not my own. Only much later was it possible to see that the journey in search of God, and the path to my true self, were the same. With this came acknowledgement that silence and solitude are necessary for all who wish to travel these depths, because without them awareness is so easily lost in the concerns of life.

The process of healing is long for most of us, but we know it has begun when, even if only spasmodically, darkness becomes a friend, filled with Divine presence. The thought germinates that everything can become a source of grace, and our real wound – whatever we may complain of – lies in our need for this Divine company. This is very counter-cultural. The society in which we live sees weakness and any type of suffering as the lessening of a person, a movement from gain to loss or from success to failure.

Why was it then, that when visiting a Tymawr Sister days away from death, lying helplessly in bed and ministered to by others, it seemed that this was the height of her vocation? W H Vanstone, past Canon Emeritus of Chester Cathedral is very helpful in his book *The Stature of Waiting*. Here he shows that our meaning lies not only in activity but in what we receive while being waited on by another to meet our need. This waiting is not only seen as a definition of the word 'patient' but applied to the experience of Jesus. He follows his descent from active life to 'the one who is done to' explaining the word 'passion' as not necessarily meaning pain but dependence on others and not being in control. This transition of Jesus, from Gethsemane onwards, was no diminishment of his calling but the high spot of his life of service.

How can this be? Vanstone explains that while he was waited on by others, Jesus reveals to us a God who waits: who waits on the world in love for a response, as all lovers do. The special dignity of man lies in the presence within him of the image of this God. So we must not see it as degrading to be waited on by others in this way, to be helped, to be dependent. For it is then that we become what God allows himself to be and, paradoxically, it is perhaps then that we are at our most Christ-like. Is this what I recognised in the Tymawr Sister?

My mother has died and the long years of diminishment and suffering are over. It was the long goodbye, but the last twelve days, spent constantly at her bedside, was a grace to hold close for ever. A very special time, it was a privilege to be with her as a midwife in reverse, aware of a deep presence in the room waiting on her. Never having completely bonded in life, we were now able to respond openly to each other. We were both embraced by the same love and free to express our love for each other. Even as she saw me as her mother (our roles were reversed), I sang for her and held her hand, while the darkness of these days was not black but dazzling.

December

LOVE

YOURS FOR THE TAKING

Gently, O so gently
you have broken through
my defences, and over the years
have removed the obstacles
put in the way
of my loving you.

But here,
with nowhere to hide,
(nor would I wish to!)
I sense the sweet smile
of your presence
in the stillness of this place.

Never less alone
than alone with you
I return your smile,
accepting your love for me
and trust you
with my whole heart
which is yours for the taking.

The garden has an ethereal feel today, as I walk the path in the light of early morning. Leaving the cottage, which is already decorated for the festivities, I pass through the half-light of awareness into the stillness and mystery of the Christmas story. With heart responding to the vulnerability of a newly-born baby, wonder rises with thought of the Divine choosing to expose himself to his own creation. You couldn't make it up! Wise men set out looking for the extraordinary, and discover it swaddled in the ordinary. All so different from what was expected!

I think of Mother Julian, the fourteenth-century hermit of Norwich, whose revelation was 'Love was His meaning', and I recognise this energy of love, not only born in this baby at Bethlehem, but let loose through all creation, including in the pattern of transformation in my own life. From here I can see both the inner and outer lives of all of us pervaded by love, even when it is not felt and not recognised. And I see this love that brought everything into being, longing for relationship with its own creation. It would seem we are specifically set up for this, with love being our deepest desire as well as source of our pain.

A poster on our church door for Christmastide shows a new baby grasping his mother's finger. The caption below is a quotation from C S Lewis: 'Love anything at all and your heart will surely be wrung and possibly broken. If you want to keep it intact, you must give your heart to no one, not even an animal.' One parishioner was heard to remark 'That's the biggest argument against Christianity I have ever heard!' It is, of course, initially scary, because it involves, on both the human and Divine level, a letting go of control and surrendering our well-being into the hands of another. A risky business!

As I think about this, about our response to love, my attention is drawn to a lone coot trying to swim up river against the pull of the tide. Watching his futile paddling the scene becomes an icon, as I realise a new awareness of the term 'surrender' is forming in relation to love. For years I alternately accepted or struggled with Jean Pierre de Caussade's poem, 'I abandon myself into your hands'. I see now that at an earlier stage of life this involved a certain amount of handing-over responsibility for myself, because of being unable to cope.

Life since has been gradually learning to take that responsibility, and yet there is a truth hidden here deeper than any misconception of mine. We have acknowledged that when we are in love, that love makes us vulnerable, and that is because we place our well-being in the hands of another. It is how the world works and helps us appreciate the motivation of the founding Cistercian Fathers 'to comfort the wounded heart of Christ'. So, at some point, whether or not it is conscious, a surrender is involved, not in the sense of giving up and showing the white flag, but opening up and relaxing inwardly. Mother Mary-Jean used to have a photograph on her desk of our four-year-old granddaughter, running through the convent cornfield with arms outstretched. She said, 'it reminds me how to live'. So, today abandonment is seen as saying 'Yes' to love and to life as it flows through all our experiences, trying not to be like the coot, but making a decision to trust the river and go with its flow. A card from a friend, entitled Zen Dog, has the sketch of a dog paddling a boat. I love the wisdom that follows – 'He knows not where he's going, for the ocean will decide; it's not the destination but the glory of the ride!'

This is all so much easier in the second half of life, when we are not trying to create our own reality. Then it becomes possible to adopt the maxim of Dag Hammarskjold:

> For all that has been, thank you
> For all that shall be, yes!

Sometimes we can only accept parts of life in retrospect, and I am confident my latent 'thank you' is heard as I look back, regretting nothing in the process of becoming fully human. Prompted to explain a little of how the *poustinia* became a reality for me, this has given me an opportunity to look back and acknowledge life's darkness as well as light. Through small windows of remembrance I can recognise a gentle, healing transformation taking place over the years at the hands of love. It was a long journey from the psychiatric wards of younger years to the present peace of the *poustinia*, but now there is awareness that not only is there treasure at the bottom of my garden but I am part of that treasure – as are you. Ours is a story of transformation even when not recognised for, if we will allow it, love flows through our daily lives unnoticed, somehow healing our divided selves through the process of living. It is true that 'suffering is the teacher of transformation' but 'the ultimate lesson is always resurrection'. (Richard Rohr)

> There is no path,
> the path is made as we go,
> the pebbles carried
> from the wild places of his love,
> with bruised hearts and bleeding fingers,
> each one given
> fond-furthering our footsteps,
> helping us home
> to the waiting heart of the Father.

BIBLIOGRAPHY

Poustinia, Catherine de Hueck Doherty, Ave Maria Press, Indiana, USA, 1975.

Traditions of Christian Spirituality, Peter-Damian Belisle OSB Cam, Orbis Books, New York and Darton, Longman & Todd, London, 2003.

The Alchemist, Paul Coelho, Harper Collins, London, 1995.

Spiritual Gardening, Peg Streep, Time-Life Custom Publishing, Alexandria, Virginia, 1999.

Falling Upwards, Richard Rohr, SPCK, London, 2012.

The Silent Land, Martin Laird, Darton, Longman & Todd, London, 2006.

The Little Prince, Antoine de Saint Exupéry, Reynal & Hitchcock, USA, 1943.

Honest to God, John Robinson, SCM Press, London, 1963.

The True Wilderness, Harry Williams, Constable & Company 1965, Fontana Paperbacks, Collins, 1976.

Tensions, Harry Williams, Mitchell Beazley Publishers, London, 1976.

Pilgrim at Tinker Creek, Anne Dillard, Harper & Row, New York, 1974.

The Cave of the Heart, Shirley du Boulay, Orbis Books, New York, 2005.

Gift from the Sea, Anne Morrow Lindbergh, Pantheon Books (a division of Random House), New York, 1955.

Eat, Pray, Love, Elizabeth Gilbert, Bloomsbury Publishing, New York, 2006.

Wisdom Jesus, Cynthia Bourgeault, Shambhala Publications, Boston, Massachusetts, 2008.

Jesus – an Historical Approximation, Jose Pagola, transl. Margaret Wilde, 4th printing, Convivium Press, Miami, Florida, 2013.

Blue Sky God, Don MacGregor, Circle Books, Aylesford, Hants, 2012.

The Practice of the Presence of God, Brother Lawrence, transl. E M Blaiklock 1981, Hodder & Stoughton, London, 1992.

The Sacrament of the Present Moment, Jean-Pierre de Caussade SJ, Desclée de Brouwer 1966, transl. Kitty Muggeridge, Fount Paperbacks, Collins, London 1981.

The Stature of Waiting, W H Vanstone, Darton, Longman & Todd, London, 1982.